W9-BVM-520

WITHDRAWN

EDGE BOOKS™

EQUIPPED FOR BATTLE

WEAPONS, GEAR, AND UNIFORMS
⇥ OF THE ⇤
CIVIL WAR

by Eric Fein

Consultant:
Jennifer L. Jones
Chair, Armed Forces History
NMAH, Smithsonian Institution
Washington, D.C.

CAPSTONE PRESS
a capstone imprint

Edge Books are published by Capstone Press,
1710 Roe Crest Drive, North Mankato, Minnesota 56003.
www.capstonepub.com

Books published by Capstone Press are manufactured with paper
containing at least 10 percent post-consumer waste.

Library of Congress Cataloging-in-Publication Data
Fein, Eric.
    Weapons, gear, and uniforms of the Civil War / by Eric Fein.
    p. cm.—(Edge books. Equipped for battle)
    Includes bibliographical references and index.
    Summary: "Describes the uniforms, gear, and weapons used by Union and Confederate
forces during the American Civil War"—Provided by publisher.
    Audience: Grades 4-6.
    ISBN 978-1-4296-7648-9 (library binding)
    1. United States—History—Civil War, 1861–1865—Equipment and supplies—Juvenile
literature. 2. United States. Army—Equipment—History—19th century—Juvenile literature.
3. Confederate States of America. Army—Equipment—History—19th century—Juvenile
literature. 4. Military weapons—United States—History—19th century—Juvenile literature.
I. Title. II. Series.
E491.F45 2012
973.7"8—dc23   **3 9957 00169 9780**   2011028682

Editorial Credits
Aaron Sautter, editor; Ted Williams, designer; Eric Manske, production specialist

Photo Credits
Alamy: Classic Image, 9 (top), 11 (right), North Wind Picture Archives, cover (battle);
CorbisRF, 23 (bottom); Corbis: Bettmann, 12, 25 (bottom), 26, Bettmann/Mathew B.
Brady, 11 (left), Medford Historical Society Collection/Andrew J. Russell, 22 (bottom);
Getty Images: Buyenlarge, 15 (bottom), 27 (bottom), Hulton Archive, 25 (top), MPI, 27
(top), Photoquest, 28; iStockphoto: Charles Knox, 22 (top), Getty Images/MPI/Hulton
Archive, 4-5; James P. Rowan, 16 (top), 17 (bottom), 19 (bottom), 20 (top), 23 (top, middle),
29 (bottom); Ketchum Hand Grenade WICR 30377 in the collection of Wilson's Creek
National Battlefield, 21 (top); Library of Congress, cover (soldier); Painting by Don Troiani,
www.historicalimagebank.com, 8, 9 (bottom), 10; Shutterstock/HHsu, cover (cannon); Super
Stock Inc.: Science and Society, 29 (top); Wikipedia: Hmaag, 18, (both) 19 (top); www.
historicalimagebank.com, 13 (both), 14 (both), 15 (top), 16 (bottom), 17 (top), 20 (bottom),
Connecticut Museum of History, 21 (bottom), West Point Museum, 24

Artistic Effects
iStockphoto: Duncan Walker, Leslie Banks; Shutterstock: caesart, Ewa Walicka, maigi,
Oleg Golovnev

Printed in the United States of America in Stevens Point, Wisconsin.
102011   006404WZS12

TABLE OF CONTENTS

→ WAR BETWEEN ← THE STATES

In the early morning hours of April 12, 1861, heavy guns pounded Fort Sumter near Charleston, South Carolina. It was just the beginning of the bloodiest war in U.S. history. The U.S. Civil War (1861–1865) grew out of tensions concerning the end of slavery and keeping the country together. The Southern states' economy was based on farming and slavery. African-Americans had been held in slavery in the South for nearly 250 years.

The Northern states' economy was based on industrial manufacturing. Slaves weren't used in the factories. Many northerners felt slavery was wrong and should be stopped. But people in the South didn't want to free their slaves. They believed that states had the right to choose to be a slave state or a free state. Many heated debates took place in the U.S. Congress. People from the North and the South argued about slavery and states' rights for several years.

Beginning in 1860, several states chose to **secede** from the United States. They formed a new country called the Confederate States of America. However, President Abraham Lincoln wanted to keep the United States together as one nation. For the next four years, Union and Confederate soldiers fought a terrible war that cost more than half a million American lives.

secede—to withdraw from a group or organization

FIVE MAJOR CIVIL WAR BATTLES

- **Battle of Shiloh, Tennessee**
  Fought: April 6–7, 1862
  Union casualties: 13,047
  Confederate casualties: 10,694

- **Battle of Antietam, Maryland**
  Fought: September 17, 1862
  Union casualties: 12,410
  Confederate casualties: 13,724

- **Battle of Chancellorsville, Virginia**
  Fought: April 27–May 6, 1863
  Union casualties: 16,845
  Confederate casualties: 12,764

- **Battle of Gettysburg, Pennsylvania**
  Fought: July 1–3, 1863
  Union casualties: 23,055
  Confederate casualties: 28,063

- **Battle of Chickamauga, Georgia**
  Fought: August 16–September 22, 1863
  Union casualties: 16,170
  Confederate casualties: 18,454

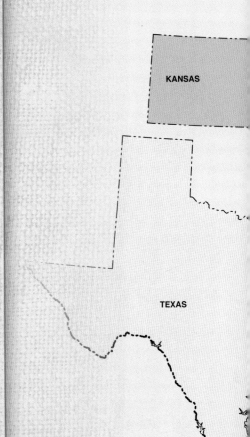

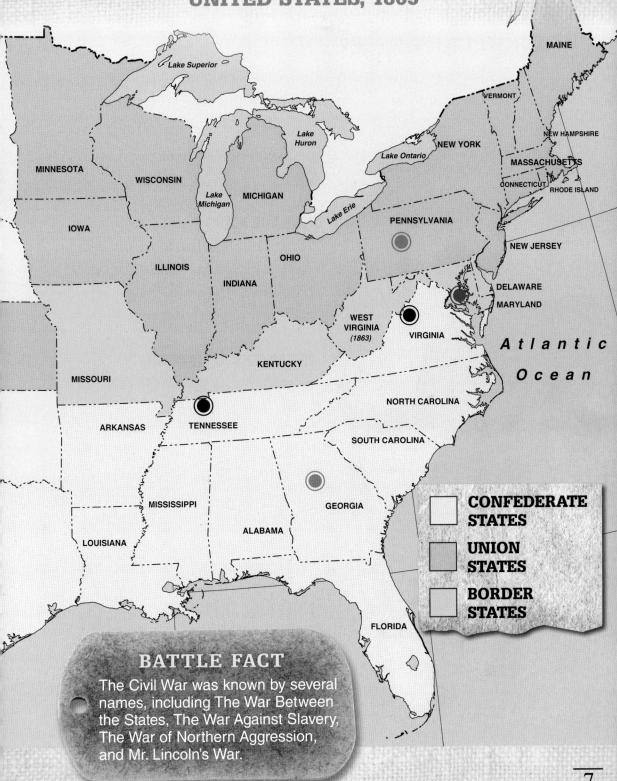

UNITED STATES, 1865

MAINE

Lake Superior

VERMONT

NEW HAMPSHIRE

Lake Huron

NEW YORK

Lake Ontario

MINNESOTA

WISCONSIN

MASSACHUSETTS

CONNECTICUT

RHODE ISLAND

Lake Michigan

MICHIGAN

Lake Erie

IOWA

PENNSYLVANIA

NEW JERSEY

ILLINOIS

OHIO

DELAWARE

INDIANA

MARYLAND

WEST VIRGINIA *(1863)*

VIRGINIA

Atlantic

Ocean

KENTUCKY

MISSOURI

NORTH CAROLINA

ARKANSAS

TENNESSEE

SOUTH CAROLINA

MISSISSIPPI

GEORGIA

ALABAMA

LOUISIANA

	CONFEDERATE STATES
	UNION STATES
	BORDER STATES

FLORIDA

BATTLE FACT

The Civil War was known by several names, including The War Between the States, The War Against Slavery, The War of Northern Aggression, and Mr. Lincoln's War.

→ UNIFORMS ←

UNION UNIFORMS

A soldier's weapons, clothing, and gear were key to surviving the war. The Union army's dress code detailed the style, color, and type of clothes soldiers wore. Each branch of the military used slightly different versions of a standard uniform.

FORAGE CAPS

Most Union **infantry** soldiers wore a forage cap made from dark blue wool. They were based on a French military hat called a kepi.

INFANTRY UNIFORMS

Union officers and soldiers were given long wool dress coats. But many soldiers preferred wearing more comfortable sack coats. These short coats had a turnover collar and an inside left pocket. Soldiers also wore light blue pants, a dark wool shirt, socks, long underwear, and tough leather shoes.

UNIFORM BUTTONS

Buttons were often stamped with an eagle with spread wings. Officers' buttons were marked with I, C, or A, which stood for Infantry, **Cavalry**, or Artillery.

→ **infantry**—a group of soldiers trained to fight and travel on foot

CAVALRY SOLDIER UNIFORMS

Union cavalry uniform pants were reinforced in the seat and inside legs to prevent wear and tear from the saddle. Overcoats were made with a slit up the back to make riding and dismounting easier.

SLEEVE RANK BRAIDS

A Union officer's rank was shown with knotted braids on the sleeves of his overcoat. The rank of general had five braids in a double knot. A captain had two braids in a single knot.

BERDAN'S SHARPSHOOTERS

In 1861 Hiram Berdan formed the Sharpshooters. They were a group of expert marksmen known for their accurate shooting. They were nicknamed the "Green Coats" because they wore dark green coats. They also wore green pants.

→ **cavalry**—a group of soldiers who fight and travel on horseback

CONFEDERATE UNIFORMS

At the start of the war, most Confederate soldiers didn't have official uniforms. The South didn't have factories to mass-produce uniforms. Soldiers often wore locally made clothing instead. Confederate uniforms were many different colors at first. A yellow-brown color called "butternut" was common. Later in the war, Confederate jackets were almost always gray.

INFANTRY UNIFORMS

The Southern uniform code originally called for a long gray coat. However, a short, waist-length coat replaced it. Confederate troops were sometimes called "graybacks." Soldiers usually wore gray, yellow-brown, or blue pants. They also had white cotton shirts, socks, and leather shoes. Some wore a forage cap.

BATTLE FACT

Confederate soldiers often had trouble getting quality clothes. Many took uniforms off dead Union soldiers or from Union prisoners. They sometimes dyed Union uniforms to avoid being mistaken for a Union soldier.

CAVALRY SOLDIERS

Confederate cavalry units often did not follow an official dress code. Their clothes were usually plain gray or butternut in color.

BELT BUCKLES

Confederate belts often had oval-shaped belt plates. Confederate belts usually used the Confederate States' initials, C.S. However, some Confederate troops wore buckles that had their home state's initials on them.

ZOUAVE SOLDIERS

Both Union and Confederate armies had Zouave soldiers. These soldiers were specially trained with new combat methods that made them efficient in battle. Both Union and Confederate Zouaves wore bright-colored uniforms, baggy pants, and a forage cap.

Civil War soldiers carried much more than their weapons. They had to pack and carry all the gear they used daily. Soldiers carried their tents, blankets, canteens, and other necessities as they marched between battles.

HEAVY EQUIPMENT

Fully equipped soldiers had to carry 40 to 50 pounds (18 to 23 kilograms) of gear. Soldiers carried food, ponchos, mess kits, and personal items in a knapsack.

CONFEDERATE "BLANKETS"

Confederate soldiers often did not have blankets. Many used old carpet pieces as blankets instead.

CANTEENS

Union canteens were made from two dish-shaped parts that were welded together. They were covered in cloth and had a leather or canvas strap. Many Union canteens held close to 3 pints (1.4 liters) of water. Confederate troops often carried canteens made from wood.

CARTRIDGE BOXES

Cartridge boxes were made from black leather. Inside were two tin compartments that held 40 black gunpowder cartridges. When filled, cartridge boxes weighed more than 3 pounds (1.4 kg). Soldiers carried the boxes on a waist belt.

IDENTITY DISCS

Union soldiers were not given official dog tags for identification. Instead, some soldiers bought identity discs that were made by jewelers. The discs were often advertised in newspapers or sold by civilian army suppliers called sutlers.

BATTLE FACT

Many soldiers could not afford identity discs. Instead, they simply wrote their names on a piece of paper. Soldiers would pin the papers onto their coats before going into battle.

CIVIL WAR FOOD

Most soldiers ate a simple diet. They lived on bread, bacon, beans, dried potatoes, coffee, and sugar. They ate beef occasionally. However, the meat was often rotten and crawling with maggots. Soldiers also ate a tough crackerlike bread called hardtack.

GUM BLANKETS

A gum blanket was a piece of cloth coated with rubber. Soldiers usually used it as a rain cape. It could also be used as a floor for a small shelter called a pup tent. Soldiers sometimes drew game boards on them for playing games such as checkers.

MESS KITS

Soldiers were given mess kits by their home states. Each state had its own mess kit design. Mess kits usually included forks, spoons, knives, plates, and cups. A few included salt and pepper shakers.

McCLELLAN CAVALRY SADDLES

Union General George McClellan designed his own saddle before the war. The McClellan saddle was one of the most popular during the war. It was lightweight, sturdy, and inexpensive.

TENTS

Soldiers used various tents for shelter. A poncho tent was made with three rubber-coated blankets. It could hold three soldiers. Pup tents were not well-liked by most soldiers. They got their name because they were very small. Soldiers complained that only a small dog could stay dry in one.

RIFLES

At the start of the Civil War, many troops used basic muskets. They were inaccurate and often didn't hit their targets. But advances were made during the war. Rifles were faster to load than muskets. And they were more accurate. The new rifle designs helped soldiers shoot more enemies from a greater distance.

1861 SPRINGFIELD RIFLE

The Springfield was one of the most common rifles used in the war. The gun weighed about 9 pounds (4 kg) and was nearly 5 feet (1.5 meters) long. A **bayonet** could be attached to the end, making the weapon more than 6 feet (1.8 m) long.

SHARPS RIFLE AND CARBINE

Sharps rifles and carbines were used mostly by Union soldiers. Troops could quickly load and fire these **breech**-loading guns. The rifle was 47 inches (119 centimeters) long and weighed 8.75 pounds (3.9 kg). The carbine was 39 inches (99 cm) long and weighed about 8 pounds (3.6 kg).

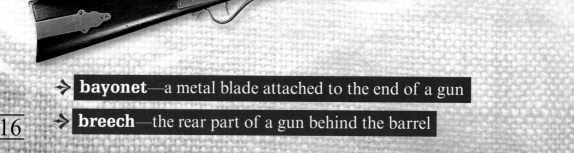

→ **bayonet**—a metal blade attached to the end of a gun

→ **breech**—the rear part of a gun behind the barrel

ENFIELD RIFLE MUSKET 1853

Both the Confederate and Union armies used Enfield rifles. The Enfield was made in England and imported to the United States. It weighed about 9 pounds (4 kg) and had a 33-inch (84-cm) barrel.

HENRY REPEATING RIFLE

The Henry was the most advanced rifle used by the Union in the war. It weighed about 9 pounds (4 kg) and had a 24-inch (61-cm) long barrel. Its magazine held 15 rounds, which could all be fired in less than 11 seconds. It was not an official weapon. Union soldiers usually had to buy the rifle with their own money.

SPENCER RIFLE

The Spencer rifle was a seven-shot repeater rifle. It was 47 inches (119 cm) long and weighed 10 pounds (4.5 kg). A well-trained marksman could fire all seven shots in 12 seconds.

BATTLE FACT

Christopher M. Spencer invented the Spencer rifle in 1860. President Lincoln tested the rifle himself near the White House. Lincoln was impressed with the rifle's accuracy. He soon ordered as many of these weapons as Spencer's factory could provide.

HANDGUNS

Along with rifles, soldiers carried handguns. Small guns were useful when a soldier ran out of **ammunition** for his rifle. Both the Union and Confederate armies used a wide variety of handguns. Navy guns usually fired .36-caliber bullets, while army guns used .44-caliber bullets.

COLT MODEL 1851 NAVY REVOLVER

The Colt 1851 Navy revolver was made from 1850 to 1873. It was a .36-caliber revolver that held six shots. Its 7.5-inch (19-cm) barrel was shaped like an octagon.

COLT MODEL 1861 NAVY REVOLVER

The 1861 revolver was identical to the Model 1851, except that its barrel was round.

SHOULDER STOCKS

Colt made shoulder stock attachments for some of their handguns. A shoulder stock helped make a gun more stable as it was fired. The Model 1851 came with a shoulder stock that contained a canteen.

ammunition—bullets and other objects fired from weapons

COLT MODEL 1860 ARMY REVOLVER

The 1860 Army revolver was a six shot
.44-caliber handgun. The dependable weapon
was the main handgun used by Union troops.
It was about 14 inches (36 cm) long.

LeMAT "GRAPESHOT" REVOLVER

The LeMat revolver was mainly used by the Confederate
army. It had two barrels. The secondary **smoothbore**
barrel could fire a shotgun load of small pellets. The gun was
known as the "Grapeshot" revolver because of this feature.

AUGUSTA MACHINE WORKS REVOLVER

The Confederacy didn't have many real Colt revolvers. Instead, they
copied the pattern without Colt's approval. The end result was a
nearly identical gun called the Augusta Machine Works revolver.

 smoothbore—having a smooth
surface on the inside of a gun's barrel

BLADES AND GRENADES

Civil War soldiers also used swords, bayonets, and grenades in battle. However, both sides quickly learned that edged weapons were of little use against guns. Soldiers often used their blades for everyday tasks instead, such as opening cans or holding meat over an open fire. Sometimes bayonets were even used as stakes or pins for soldiers' tents.

LIGHT CAVALRY SABER MODEL 1860

This sword's blade was 34 inches (86 cm) long and was slightly curved. The weapon had a hand guard made of brass. The grip was covered in black leather that was tied with brass wire.

CONFEDERATE SWORD

Confederate swords were usually copies of Union swords. However, they were often made from low-quality materials.

CONFEDERATE BAYONETS

Like many Confederate weapons, Southern bayonets were copies of Union models. But the quality was not as good. Some bayonets had steel only in their tips. The rest of the blades were made from iron, which could break easily.

KETCHUM'S GRENADE

The Ketchum's grenade came in 1-, 3-, and 5-pound (0.5-, 1.4-, and 2.3-kg) sizes. It had a wooden tail with cardboard fins to help it land and explode correctly.

HAYNES "EXCELSIOR" HAND GRENADE

The Haynes grenade was a cast-iron ball with an inner and an outer shell. The inner shell held the explosive powder. The Haynes was made to explode on impact after being thrown. Its outer shell would explode into deadly fragments.

Armies pounded enemy troops with artillery weapons such as cannons, mortars, and howitzers during the war. These guns were large and heavy. It took a small group of soldiers to move, load, and fire these powerful weapons. The guns could fire large ammunition to destroy enemy targets from long distances.

12-POUNDER NAPOLEON MODEL 1857

Both the Union and Confederacy used the Napoleon cannon. It weighed 1,227 pounds (557 kg), not including the two-wheeled carriage it sat on. The Napoleon could fire twice per minute, and it could hit targets nearly 1 mile (1.6 kilometers) away.

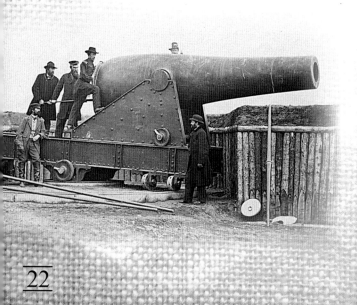

THOMAS J.RODMAN SMOOTHBORE COLUMBIAD

The Thomas J. Rodman Columbiad was one of the largest cannons ever made. It weighed 117,000 pounds (53,000 kg). The huge gun could fire a 1,080-pound (490-kg) shell at targets up to 4.5 miles (7.2 km) away.

10-POUNDER PARROTT

The Parrott cannon had a **rifled** cast-iron tube. An iron hoop strengthened the breech at the rear of the gun.

WHITWORTH 12-POUNDER

The Whitworth cannon was mainly used by the Confederacy. It fired an unusual six-sided shell called a "bolt." The gun's unique shells and design made it very accurate.

MORTARS

Mortars were made to sit low to the ground. They fired heavy balls high into the sky. The ammunition then landed and exploded behind enemy lines. Mortars were used at both the battles of Vicksburg and Petersburg.

rifled—having spiraled grooves inside a gun's barrel to make bullets travel more accurately

STAKE TORPEDO

The stake **torpedo** was a land mine that held about 50 pounds (23 kg) of explosive powder. It was positioned at an angle and held in place with an anchor attached to its upper end.

GRAPESHOT/CANISTER SHOT

Two of the deadliest forms of cannon ammunition were canister and grapeshot. A tin canister was filled with 27 cast-iron balls, each weighing about 0.5 pound (0.23 kg). The canister was then fired from a smoothbore cannon. Grapeshot included nine large iron balls wrapped in cloth or canvas.

BATTLE FACT

Land torpedoes were like modern-day land mines. Known as "sensitive shells," they were usually buried in the ground and exploded when stepped on.

COAL TORPEDO

Coal torpedoes were actually small bombs. Hollow pieces of iron were filled with explosive powder. Then they were covered in tar and coal dust to look like coal. They were hidden in coal depots where Union ships got the coal to power their engines. When the torpedoes were thrown into a ship's furnace, they would explode and damage the ship.

torpedo—a stationary mine or bomb used in the Civil War

SWAMP ANGEL CANNON

The Union used this big Parrott cannon to attack the city of Charleston, South Carolina, on August 22, 1863. The gun fired 200-pound (91-kg) shells from a floating platform on a marsh at the mouth of Charleston Harbor.

WHISTLING DICK

The Whistling Dick had a rifled barrel. It got its nickname from the sound its ammunition made. The 18-pound (8-kg) shell made a whistling sound as it flew through the air.

UNION AND CONFEDERATE NAVIES

In 1861 both the Union and Confederacy had only a few ships. But by the end of the war, the Union had 671 ships, while the Confederacy had about 500 vessels. Both sides also began making ironclad ships. These warships were covered with sheets of iron armor to protect against enemy fire.

CSS *VIRGINIA*

From 1861 to 1862, the South rebuilt the wrecked Union ship USS *Merrimack* into the ironclad battleship the CSS *Virginia*. It was about 263 feet (80 meters) long. It had 10 heavy guns. It was the first ironclad ship made by the Confederacy.

BATTLE FACT

The *Monitor* and the *Virginia* clashed on March 9, 1862. It was the first battle between two ironclad warships. The battle was fought to a draw.

USS *MONITOR*

The USS *Monitor* was the first ironclad ship built by the Union. It was 179 feet (55 m) long. It sat low in the water, with only about 18 inches (46 cm) of the hull above the water's surface. It had a turret on top that contained two powerful 11-inch (28-cm) guns.

CSS *H. L. HUNLEY* SUBMARINE

The Confederate submarine CSS *H. L. Hunley* was made in part from an old boiler. It was about 40 feet (12 m) long and about 4 feet (1.2 m) wide. It was powered manually by eight men sitting at eight cranks on the end of a propeller shaft. The *H. L. Hunley* is known as the first submarine to sink an enemy ship during wartime.

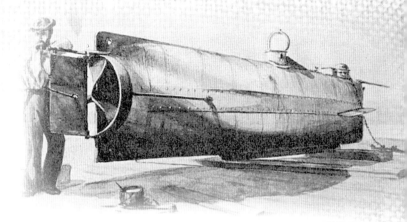

UNION GUNBOATS

Union gunboats patrolled rivers. The boats were powered by side-wheels that allowed them to move through shallow river waters. Gunboats were heavily armed with cannons. Many were covered with armor 1.5 to 2 inches (3.8 to 5 cm) thick. A few gunboats had poor armor and were called "tinclads."

MACHINE GUNS, VOLLEY GUNS, AND ROCKETS

Machine guns and rockets were introduced during the Civil War but were not widely used. Early machine guns often became jammed and had other malfunctions. And rockets could be unpredictable.

BILLINGHURST-REQUA BATTERY GUN

The Billinghurst-Requa was made from 25 rifle barrels placed side by side on a wooden frame. It was carried on a lightweight carriage. It was called a covered bridge gun because it was often used to defend covered bridges.

AGER "COFFEE MILL" MACHINE GUN

The Ager machine gun was nicknamed the "Coffee Mill." It used a hand crank that looked similar to the kind used on coffee grinders at the time. The gun could fire 120 rounds per minute.

GATLING GUN

The Gatling gun had six barrels that rotated with a crank. It could fire more than 200 rounds per minute.

HALE ROCKET

The Hale rocket had three curved vanes at its base to make it spin while in flight. The spinning motion kept it stable as it flew. It could travel up to 1 mile (1.6 km).

WILLIAMS "ONE-POUNDER" MACHINE GUN

The Williams machine gun could fire 65 1-pound (0.5-kg) rounds per minute. It had a range of 2,000 yards (1,829 m). This gun was used in the Battle of Seven Pines in 1862.

VANDENBERG VOLLEY GUN

The Vandenberg volley gun was developed during the war, but saw little use. It had between 85 to 451 barrels. The number of barrels depended on the size of ammunition being used. The weapon was fired by a charge that set off all the barrels at the same time.

GLOSSARY

ammunition (am-yuh-NI-shuhn)—bullets and other objects that can be fired from weapons

bayonet (BAY-uh-net)—a long metal blade attached to the end of a musket or rifle

breech (BREECH)—the rear part of a gun behind the gun's barrel

cartridge (KAHR-trij)—a tube containing the gunpowder, primer, and a bullet for a gun

cavalry (KA-vuhl-ree)—a group of soldiers who travel and fight on horseback

infantry (IN-fuhn-tree)—a group of soldiers trained to fight and travel on foot

rifled (RYE-fuhld)—having spiraled grooves inside the barrel of a gun to make bullets travel more accurately

secede (si-SEED)—to formally withdraw from a group or organization, often to form a new organization

smoothbore (SMOOTH-bohr)—having a smooth surface on the inside of a gun's barrel

torpedo (tor-PEE-doh)—a stationary mine or explosive device

READ MORE

Olson, Kay Melchisedech. *The Terrible, Awful Civil War: The Disgusting Details about Life During America's Bloodiest War.* Disgusting History. Mankato, Minn.: Capstone Press, 2010.

Roche, Tim. *Soldiers of the Civil War.* Why We Fought: The Civil War. Chicago: Heinemann Library, 2011.

Stanchak, John. *Eyewitness Civil War.* DK Eyewitness Books. New York: Dorling Kindersley, 2011.

INTERNET SITES

FactHound offers a safe, fun way to find Internet sites related to this book. All of the sites on FactHound have been researched by our staff.

Here's all you do:

Visit *www.facthound.com*

Type in this code: 9781429676489

Super-cool stuff!

Check out projects, games and lots more at
www.capstonekids.com

INDEX